Treasurer of Piggy Banks

Literary Activism

Series Editor: Amit Chaudhuri

Treasurer of Piggy Banks

Vinod Kumar Shukla

Translated from Hindi by
Arvind Krishna Mehrotra

Published by Westland Books, a division of Nasadiya Technologies Private Limited, in 2024

No. 269/2B, First Floor, 'Irai Arul', Vimalraj Street, Nethaji Nagar, Alapakkam Main Road, Maduravoyal, Chennai 600095

Westland and the Westland logo are the trademarks of Nasadiya Technologies Private Limited, or its affiliates.

ISBN:

10 9 8 7 6 5 4 3 2 1

Typeset by Jojy Philip, New Delhi

Printed at [⊠]

Contents

A Note on the Series

'Literary activism' is a project that began in 2014 with a series of annual symposia. Its aim was to create a space for the kind of discussion on creativity no longer available in mainstream contexts (literary festivals, book launches) or in academic ones (conferences, classrooms, monographs). The literary activism website—literaryactivism.com—was created in 2020, and the Centre for the Creative and the Critical at Ashoka University came into existence in 2022 at Ashoka University to give this project a home, and to look at the kind of thinking that writing and the arts comprise.

This new imprint, 'literary activism', is meant to carry forward these ambitions in the realm of publishing. The art vs science debate is now a historical relic, but what interests us is the possibility of creating a meaning for writing that's separate from market value and academic legitimacy. And we wish to recall that art and writing are not synonymous with the generalised academic discipline called the 'humanities': they have an angularity to it, and to the social science perspectives the humanities are now subsumed under. The 'literary activism' imprint wishes not only to publish good writing, but to pursue this angularity.

Grass Lives Next to Grass

Arvind Krishna Mehrotra

> Writing a poem,
> worldly matters occupy me.[1]

Thus begins a poem by Vinod Kumar Shukla. By 'worldly matters', you would have thought Shukla meant political disputes, grocery shopping, landlords, the weather, train timetables. As it turns out, at least in this instance, it is none of the above, though all of the above figure in his work. 'If I'm writing,' the poem continues,

> and there's a knock on the door,
> I go open it
> when I hear the sound.

It's a short poem, and I've already quoted two of its four stanzas. The poem was written in 2008.

Sometime in 1970, there was a knock on Shukla's door. The person knocking had been specially sent to fetch Shukla's manuscript for a poetry series that Ashok Vajpeyi, whom Shukla knew, was bringing out. Vajpeyi, a civil servant, was at the time posted in Sarguja, a district to the north of Raipur where Shukla lives, and his letter asking for the manuscript—and sent in his capacity as a poet, critic, and, now, editor of poetry chapbooks—had gone unanswered. Shukla's poems, which had been appearing in Hindi literary magazines since 1959, were to be part of the series, if only Shukla would cooperate.

The chapbook eventually appeared and was titled *Lagbhag Jai Hind* [*Hail India, Almost*]. The phrase 'Jai Hind', which translates as 'Hail India' or 'Long live India', had been a stirring political slogan from pre-Independence times. The irony of the 'Almost'—especially at a time when the nation was newly independent—marked Shukla out as someone who stood at a slight angle to a rallying cry meant to give goosebumps. It's a bit like having the second line of 'Hail to the Chief!' read 'Hail to the Chief! We almost salute him, one and all.' Vajpeyi's chapbooks appeared under the series title Pehchan [Sign]. For Shukla, Pehchan was particularly apt.

In the poems of *Lagbhag Jai Hind* are lines like, 'This flock of ducks/was like a duck./It had a duck's bill and wings' and 'Six in the morning was like six in the morning.' The lines are unique to Shukla, like a fingerprint. You could put them on a cheque and it would be honoured at any literary bank. Similar, even identical, sentences occur in his prose as well. 'The crowd was like a crowd', 'Blue is like blue', and 'The flock of ducks looked like ducks. They had ducks' bills and feathers' are from his story 'Man in the Blue Shirt' in which the narrator sees a man—the man in the blue shirt—walking in the same direction twice, but he hadn't seen him returning after the first time he went. 'I am sure it was the same man,' the narrator says. In another story, a man has two noses.

A thing, a person, a thought is incomparably itself, inhabiting its own starkness, untouched by the consolating diversion of metaphor. Shukla is an undescriptive poet. 'The people I met on the way were like the people one meets on the way' is from his autobiographical essay 'Old Veranda'. For Hindi readers, Shukla's self-metaphorising images have the same familiarity that Gertrude Stein's rose has for others.

Shukla's poetry and prose overlap in other ways too. 'A Poem Lived First in the Novel', the first poem in the present selection, does not appear in any of his books of poems but comes after the dedication page of *A Window Lived in the Wall* (1997), a novel dedicated to his wife. The title of the novel is then repeated in the title of a poem, 'There was a window that lived in a wall' in *Nothing Surplus* (2000).

A line of Shukla is like a line of Shukla. It 'mirrors nothing' but itself. Reading him can be disorienting, even vertiginous, like seeing Op art.

* * *

As vertiginous his work may be for the reader, if you were to ask Shukla he'll say, 'I don't have wings.' The line, from 'Do birds sitting on the ground', could be a metaphor for the kind of writing Shukla does, whether poetry or fiction. He compares, in the poem, the flight of a bird with the flight of a butterfly and concludes, 'There's a small yellow butterfly/flying above the earth.'

Smallness is the dominant feature of Shukla's work, and in his small bare pictureless rooms live modest people with vivid interior lives. In 'There was a window that lived in a wall', there's more than a window that lives in the wall. Concealed from the world there's also a man, someone like Shukla himself, living in it. He is 'so absolutely the average man', as Alfred Jarry says of Marcueil in *The Supermale*, that his very ordinariness makes him 'extraordinary'. The busy shopper of 'A street in the bazaar', his frayed bag filled with potatoes, leafy vegetables, and spices, is observed by another who wishes he were a ten-rupee note and could find shelter in that bag, away from his own anxieties. In 'Through the window screen', the room chases out the terrified occupant, unless it is the occupant who flees the room, chased by his own thoughts. And in 'To my friend I said', when friends meet they talk about 'egg stalls and fighter jets', then enter into an argument. They could have talked about anything, and argued over anything, and remained friends.

Friendships (and neighbourhoods) are important to Shukla; they help fill the emptiness of the day. You meet friends at streetcorners and shoot the breeze. In 'Continuously', the mahogany leaves fall as though they were seconds. There's little else to do except count them. To tell the time you don't have to bend your neck and consult your wristwatch but look at the tree. Addressing no one in particular,

> 'Anyone for Moti Park?' the rickshaw puller asks.
> The friend's nowhere around.

Returning from work, to brighten up their walls, fathers bring home colourful posters

... of chubby, pink-faced
children—so unlike our own,
who're neither as chubby,
nor as pretty, nor wear
such nice clothes.[2]

Not everyone lives poorly, and even the tallest of men, like others in the neighbourhood, may not be any taller than 5'6". In the Jurassic Park of humanity there are no dinosaurs:

Oi! Are these the great heights you've reached?
Mind your head and you're shorter by a few more inches.[3]

* * *

Quietly, by stealth, Shukla raises and leaves the concerns that draw him, and us, again and again. Only in our case they flicker and vanish in the mind's peripheral vision before we can quite see them. As the title poem of Shukla's first full-length collection has it, 'That man put on a new woollen coat and went away like a thought.' While the man in the woollen coat (who can stand in for the reader) disappears into the winter chill, the speaker of the poem, the one in rubber flip-flops, comes into view, along with a tree and 'a horse of inferior stock'. 'There was only one horse. I wasn't that horse,' protests the speaker, but in the eyes of the boss he is 'a horse at a gallop, horseshoes nailed to [his] boot soles.' The working man has changed places with the workhorse. The boss remains what he is, an unattainable idea of wealth, someone snug in the woollen coat of his printed thoughts.

'Worldly matters' come knocking all the time. In a bus queue you find there's a tree standing in front:

When the bus arrived
I waited for the tree to get on first when it struck me
that trees
do not board buses.[4]

Shukla's images, like the one above, only pretend to be like children's drawings. The playfulness is deceptive. The tree is trying to escape to the city before it, too, is turned into a log. 'It hasn't rained yet' begins:

> It hasn't rained yet.
> The tree in front of our house
> had been cut down.
> Is that the reason?

The absence of trees, whether 'in front of our house' or in the forest, is in the short term a portent of drought; in the long term of what has been described as a climate 'doom loop'. The word 'climate' has spawned a whole new literary genre, but this is not what Shukla is talking about. He's been living in the knot of that loop, seeing it tighten. For him the end has already come.

> O adivasis! The trees did not desert you,
> nor did you leave the forest on your own.
> I saw groups of you walking down city streets this year,
> bedraggled children in tow, forest people without forests.
> Is that the reason?
>
> The year's now ended.
> In the groups of families
> I noticed there were no infants.
> Is this the beginning
> of the end of the adivasis?

The decimation of what is euphemistically called 'first peoples' is no surprise when read about in the news or in history books. To come upon it unexpectedly, in a different context, is to make what had been forgotten or pushed to the back of our minds, resurface once again.

* * *

'There is nothing of me except what is here,' Shukla says in 'When everyone thinks I'm dead'. Shukla's 'here' is a specific place, Raipur and, before that, Rajnandgaon, both cities in Chhattisgarh, one third of whose population is adivasi. Born in Rajnandgaon in 1937, he went to school and college there. His family were Saryuparin Brahmins who hailed from Uttar Pradesh. Raipur is where he taught agricultural extension at the Indira Gandhi Agricultural University. He retired as associate professor in 1996. This is not your usual trajectory of someone who's been described as the greatest living writer in Hindi and been awarded the 2023 PEN/Nabokov Award for Achievement in International Literature, but therein lies the paradox of Vinod Kumar Shukla.

Though there was until the 1970s little to distinguish Rajnandgaon and Raipur from the other small stations on the Bombay–Howrah rail line, in Shukla's eyes they encompass the known world. The middle of nowhere is also somewhere. In 'The Chhattisgarh to Bilaspur', the Chhattisgarh Express, for part of the way, takes the same Bombay–Howrah route. Were it left to him, Shukla would still be living in the house of his childhood that he writes about in 'Old Veranda':

Ours was a family of four brothers living under one roof. The roof's shadow belonged to my youngest uncle, who was called Chachaji. He was called this at home and also outside, but wherever he was he largely kept to himself. Everyone was in awe of him. If he stepped out of the house more than he usually did, he came up against the world as if against a wall. He came up against it even when he was at home.

As happens in joint families, there would be quarrels.

Guns would come out but were never fired. The women never quarrelled. Perhaps this was because of Amma, who continued to work quietly despite the chaos of marriages, births, and deaths.

I don't know how, but her quiet would have a calming effect on those who were grieving, and those who were full of joy would find the space around them expand to accommodate their laughter.

Amma would be up when it was still dark and would be the last to sleep. You could hear her in the kitchen putting things away, the clattering sounds like a lullaby for the night, sending it to sleep. Even the plants listened to her. As soon as it was twilight, the guava, the drumstick tree, and the *tulsi* in the courtyard would doze off, as would the soft grass in the corner and the two tomato plants that had appeared on the rubbish heap. The tall peepul tree to the east of the house would look in, and seeing the other plants asleep, go to sleep itself.

If she saw an ant in the fire crawling on a dung-cake she would pull out the dung-cake and save the ant. In the same way, she would save us from small everyday fires and hope that they wouldn't recur. The burn on her hand would not have healed before she burned herself again. Her daily routine was like a thread going through the different things she did, stringing them together. She never felt the needle's prick, but I did. In the papers I read about a man who was hospitalized and discovered to have hundreds of needles in his body. Was my condition similar to that man's?[5]

The large family living under 'one roof' is an idea that he returns to in 'Would that we all had lived together'. By the time the poem ends, though, a particular family has become the human family, and the 'one roof' is not the roof of a house in Rajnandgaon but the sky. The earth we dwell on is the only mailing address we have, collectively. A particular childhood memory has here opened out into a feeling that is not dissimilar to what W.H. Auden called a 'vision of Agape', that is, of shared unerotic love. Going a step further, Shukla shares the feeling with all of creation:

> Without knots,
> there's one wind circling the earth, together with our breathing.

* * *

Apart from Gajanan Madhav Muktibodh (1917–1964), whom Shukla first met in 1958 when Muktibodh was teaching in a college in Rajnandgaon, and who suggested that Shukla send his poems to a magazine where they subsequently appeared, an influence on Shukla has been films. According to his son Shashwat Gopal, some of the names he heard from his father while growing up were Kurosawa, Tarkovsky, Satyajit Ray, Mani Kaul, and those of Iranian directors. Shukla himself has much to say on watching films in 'Old Veranda', albeit as a baby:

Krishna Talkies was inaugurated on the day I was born. The Talkies was built opposite our house. It was Rajnandgaon's first cinema hall and a big moment for the town. It's entirely possible that when, after five weeks, she [Amma] came out of the birthing room, someone who was going to see a film took me along.

Krishna Talkies was owned by the Sapre brothers. They were my father's and uncle's friends, and they may all have had some business connections as well. The ushers knew us and we had free run of the place. Krishna Talkies was almost a part of our house. When one of us, to escape from the bath that we were being subjected to in the courtyard, slipped naked through the bars of the gate and ran into the Talkies, members of the family would go in search of the chowkidar to have the gate opened. Passersby would stop to see what the fuss was about …

The third class was right up in front, where the stage and the projection screen were. Children would lie down on the stage and watch the film from there. I'd often fall asleep. Phulesar Dai would then come looking for me and carry me home. If you knock on the door of the past, the past will come out. Some of it you'll recognize. It will have its age stamped on it. It's not very remarkable to say that I spent my childhood watching the world and watching cinema. Seen from the cinema's point of view, I was just another cinemagoer.

As Shukla told an interviewer, 'My work comes to me visually.' It is no surprise, then, that Shukla's poems appear projected on the page as much as printed on it. 'Even at night in the forest'[6] is made of scenes rather than stanzas or verse paragraphs. There are in the poem, as in a film, moments of suspense. At times, you can hear the soundtrack:

> If you hear a sound
> it's probably an adivasi
> hiding to save his life
> or a man hiding
> to kill another man

Filmmakers have recognised the visual quality of Shukla's writing. His first novel, *Naukar ki kameez* (1979), was made into a film *The Servant's Shirt* (1999) by Mani Kaul, and *The Man's Woman and Other Stories* (2009) is a triptych by Amit Dutta of three Shukla stories.

* * *

At the Jaipur Literature Festival 2011, Vinod Kumar Shukla asked Sara Rai why so many people were standing in line, each clutching a book. Told that they were all waiting to have their books signed by J.M. Coetzee, Shukla looked puzzled. Hindi writers sign books, but privately, and seldom is there a line of people waiting for them to do so. Moreover, the name Coetzee meant nothing to him, nor did the names of the other world writers present on the occasion. And this despite the fact that his own books have been translated into French, Italian, and English.

One explanation for Shukla's indifference could be that he reads only in Hindi, the local language, which has over 345 million native speakers but into which little gets translated. Shukla may be quite unaware of what the poets in Slovenia are doing. Recently, when asked in an email if he was familiar with any American or European writers, for it is they who sometimes come to mind when you read him, Shukla did not evade the question. He ignored it. The question did not deserve an answer. The world's literatures are forever creating new islands on which no writer, no poem, is alone. Shukla's island neighbourhood is variously populated. Unaware of some of the variousness though he may be, it's where you will find Shukla ('There was a window that lived in a wall') and English nursery rhymes ('There was an old woman who lived in a shoe'), or Shukla ('I'm a large gathering/and I'm each person in it'[7]) and Whitman ('I am large, I contain multitudes.'), or Shukla echoing Rilke:

> Swiftly the deer runs, leaping
> as though inside
> the iron bars of a forest.
>
> The bird doesn't seem to fly
> as far as it can go, ...[8]

* * *

> His vision, from the constantly passing bars,
> has grown so weary that it cannot hold anything else.
> It seems to him there are a thousand bars;
> and behind the bars, no world.
>
> *(Rainer Maria Rilke)*[9]

* * *

> Wherever I go, I carry this inborn death with me.
> I'll save it
> for as long as I live.[10]

* * *

> I climbed this pyre, faggots piled to fearful heights,
> convinced I'd never sacrifice
> my soul's uncounted sum to gain a future.
>
> *(Rainer Maria Rilke)*[11]

Or Shukla and Jack Spicer sitting on a park bench in Vancouver, looking at sunsets:

> Where it rises in the sea,
> the sun is like a sea bird
> trying to rise,
> but with the oil on the surface
> sticking to its feathers,
> it's unable to.[12]

* * *

> Nothing but the last sun falling in the last oily water by the docks.
> They fed the lambs sugar all winter
> Nothing but that. The last sun falling in the last oily water by the docks.

(Jack Spicer)[13]

One of Spicer's 'true propositions' reads 'THAT POEMS CRY OUT TO EACH OTHER FROM A GREAT DISTANCE.'[14]

Shukla, who seldom travels and has been outside India perhaps only three or four times on literary junkets, would agree with Hazlitt that, 'Foreign travel especially makes men pedants, not artists. What we seek, we must find at home or nowhere.' Shukla must be among the few writers alive whose work has appeared in journals and anthologies where world literature is published or discussed— *Granta, Modern Poetry in Translation, Some Kind of Beautiful Signal, The Georgia Review, The Baffler, n+1*—but who has heard neither of these journals nor of world lit, a category whose centre is everywhere and periphery nowhere. In contrast to his unawareness of the term and his indifference to the subjects that keep the assembly line of global publishing moving smoothly (historical events, personal turmoil, accounts of origins and extinctions) is the attention he lavishes on the fleeting observations, thoughts, memories, and gestures that for most of us, regardless of where we live, constitute our lives. To read him is to read not a version of what is already known, but what is constantly being inscribed in and erased from the margins of our consciousness. Every once in a while, though, he casts a glance at where we're coming from ('When I went to see Bhimbetka') and where we're headed ('The dry well is dead', 'The last cheetah is dead', 'It hasn't rained yet'). Shukla is still answering the knock on the door. It's one more poem come looking for his Raipur, Chhattisgarh address.

Notes

1. 'Writing a poem', p. 129.
2. 'This colourful picture', p. 85.
3. 'There's only one tree left in the park', p. 15.
4. 'A city person', p. 43.
5. Vinod Kumar Shukla, *Blue Is Like Blue*, translation by Arvind Krishna Mehrotra and Sara Rai, pp. 105–6.
6. Not included in this selection.
7. 'Not with my own feet', p. 147.
8. 'Swiftly the deer runs, leaping', p. 65.
9. 'The Panther', *The Selected Poetry of Rainer Maria Rilke*, translation by Stephen Mitchell, p. 25
10. 'With birth is born its twin', p. 113
11. Rainer Maria Rilke, from his final notebook, translation by William Gass, *Reading Rilke*, p. 46.
12. 'The way the sun was going down', p. 49.
13. Jack Spicer, 'Seven Poems for the *Vancouver Festival*,' *My Vocabulary Did This to Me*, p. 418.
14 Ibid., p. 206.

Treasurer of Piggy Banks

उपन्यास में पहले एक कविता रहती थी

अनगिन से निकलकर एक तारा था।
एक तारा अनगिन से बाहर कैसे निकला था?
अनगिन से अलग होकर
अकेला एक
पहला था कुछ देर।
हवा का झोंका जो आया था
वह भी था अनगिन हवा के झोंकों का
पहला झोंका कुछ देर।
अनगिन से निकलकर एक लहर भी
पहली, बस कुछ पल।
अनगिन का अकेला
अनगिन अकेले अनगिन।
अनगिन से अकेली एक—
संगिनी जीवन भर।

A Poem Lived First in the Novel

From within the innumerable,
a star appeared.
How did it appear
from within the innumerable?
It stood apart. For a while, the first.
The gust that blew
was of innumerable gusts,
and for a while, the first.
Coming out of the innumerable,
even a wave,
for a while, is the first.
Alone from the innumerable, the one
who was alone in the innumerable.
From out of the innumerable
comes one partner—
for a lifetime.

लगभग जयहिन्द
(1971)

Almost Jai Hind
(1971)

घर से बाहर निकलने की गड़बड़ी में
इतना बाहर निकल आया
कि सब जगह घुसपैठिया होने की सीमा थी।
घुसपैठिया कि देशिहा!
मेरी सूरत मुझको देखती है कि बदला नहीं।
चालाकी से अपनी सूरत की फ़ोटो मैंने
खिंचवा ली थी
कि बहुरुपिया होकर भी पहिचाना जाएगा।
सब्ज़ी बाज़ार में खड़ा होकर
मैं सोचता हूँ कि विद्रोही न कहलाने के लिए
मुझे कौन-कौन सी सब्ज़ी नहीं ख़रीदनी चाहिए।
मैं हमेशा जाता हुआ दिखलाई देता हूँ।
मैं अपनी पीठ बहुत अच्छी तरह पहिचानता हूँ।

In the confusion of leaving home,
I leave it so far behind that everywhere I go
I'm seen as an infiltrator.
Infiltrator or inhabitant?
My appearance looks at me and finds me the same.
I've had it photographed so cleverly
that I'm recognised despite the mimicries.
Standing in the vegetable market,
I'm undecided about which greens to avoid
if I don't want to be called an insurgent.
I'm always seen leaving.
I know my back only too well.

(1968)

राजनैतिक बहस में सूखे को लेकर
मैंने किसी से नहीं कहा
कि नदी के किनारे से
एक झुंड चिड़िया उड़ी है—
जैसे एक लहर कई टुकड़ों में उड़ी है।
लेकिन, पड़ोसी कुर्सी पर ऊँघते हुए लोगों के बीच
बैठी हुई किसी चिड़िया को दिखलाकर मैंने हल्ला मचाया
कि टेबिल पर लहर का टुकड़ा है।
दस दोस्तों ने गाकर बताया
कि लहर का टुकड़ा खिड़की से आया।
दीवाल की खूंटी पर बैठा।
मुँह-हाथ धोना है। इत्यादि।
और लहर का चेहरा नदी से मिलता-जुलता है।
पानी से भरी बाल्टी का चेहरा नदी से मिलता-जुलता है।
संसद के कंघी के आकार के होने की प्रक्रिया में
सरकार के सिर पर बाल नहीं थे।

Turning to the drought in the political dispute,
I didn't say a word about the flock of birds
that had risen from the riverbank
like a wave rising in a thousand fragments.
But pointing to a bird in our midst,
the participants already half asleep,
I shouted and said that one of the fragments
had landed on the table.
The ten friends then sang together.
The fragment, they said, had come in
through the window;
had perched on a peg in the wall;
and they wanted to freshen up, etcetera.
The wave's face resembles a river,
and the face of a bucket of water resembles a river.
With a parliament house designed to look like a comb,
the government decided to lose its hair.

(1966)

दोस्त से मैंने कहा कि सूखी झील पर बसे हुए शहर की तरह था।
पालतू बतख का झुंड सड़क पर बाएं
पैदल चल रहा था।
लोग आ रहे थे।
मैं किसी नाव या बोट का नाम लेकर
जूते पहिने हुए था।
जूते बरसाती नहीं थे।
तैरना आता तो शायद नंगे पैर चलता
बतख के झुंड बहुत थे—
आदमियों की तरह।
बतख का झुंड
बतख की तरह था।
बतख की तरह चोंच और पंख थे।
बतखनुमा गर्दन दोस्त की थी—
लंबी लटकी हुई, उसकी ही पतलून
और क़मीज़ के झोले से बाहर
आदमी की मुट्ठी में आसानी से आ सके; गोल।
अलबत्ता क़मीज़ की जेब
एक और छोटे झोले की तरह—
दो अंडों या
दो अंडों की क़ीमत के लायक़ जगह।
मेरा दोस्त बहुत गिरता था
अंडों की दुकान और बममारक हवाई जहाज़ की हमने बहस की।

To my friend I said, 'It's like a city built on a dried-up lake bed.'
A flock of tame ducks
walked to the left of the road.
There were people arriving all the time.
I'd invoked the names of sailing boats
before putting on my shoes.
The shoes weren't waterproof.
If I knew how to swim, I wouldn't have worn them.
There were many flocks of ducks
looking like flocks of men.
This flock of ducks
was like a duck.
It had a duck's bill and wings.
The duck-like neck, though, was my friend's.
It hung out of his shirt and trousers
as if out of a bag
and would have fitted a man's grip nicely.
It was round in shape.
His shirt pocket was like a second bag.
Smaller in size, it could still hold
two eggs or the money for two eggs.
My friend was injury prone.
He and I had an argument over egg stalls and fighter jets.

(1966)

11

वह आदमी नया गरम कोट पहिन कर चला गया विचार की तरह।
रबड़ की चप्पल पहिन कर मैं पिछड़ गया।
जाड़े में उतरे हुए कपड़े का सुबह छः बजे का वक़्त
सुबह छः बजे का वक़्त, सुबह छः बजे की तरह।
पेड़ के नीचे आदमी था।
कुहरे में आदमी के धब्बे के अन्दर वह आदमी था।
पेड़ का धब्बा बिल्कुल पेड़ की तरह था।
दाहिने रद्दी नस्ल के घोड़े का धब्बा,
रद्दी नस्ल के घोड़े की तरह था।
घोड़ा भूखा था तो
उसके लिए कुहरा हवा में घास की तरह उगा था।
और कई मकान, कई पेड़, कई सड़कें इत्यादि कोई घोड़ा नहीं था।
अकेला एक घोड़ा था। मैं घोड़ा नहीं था।
लेकिन हाँफते हुए, मेरी साँस हूबहू कुहरे के नस्ल की थी।
यदि एक ही जगह पेड़ के नीचे खड़ा हुआ वह मालिक आदमी था
तो उसके लिए
मैं दौड़ता हुआ, जूते पहिने हुए था जिसमें घोड़े की तरह नाल
ठुकी थी।

That man put on a new woollen coat and went away like a thought.
In rubber flip-flops I struggled behind.
The time was six in the morning, the time of being undressed—it
    was freezing cold.
Six in the morning was like six in the morning.
There was a man standing under a tree.
In the mist it looked like he was standing inside his own blurred
    shape.
The blurred tree looked exactly like a tree.
To its right was a blurred horse of inferior stock,
looking like a horse of inferior stock.
The horse was hungry, the mist like a grassy field to him.
There were other houses, trees, roads, but no other horse.
There was only one horse. I wasn't that horse,
but my breath when I panted was indistinguishable from the mist.
If the man standing at that one spot under the tree was the boss,
then to him I was a horse at a gallop, horseshoes nailed to my boot
    soles.

(1964)

बगीचे में केवल एक ही पेड़ बचा है।
या पेड़ में पूरा बगीचा पुता है।
पेड़ जैसे कोई सरकारी घोषणा है बगीचे के लिए।
जबकि पेड़ पर चढ़ना मना है
सम्मान के लिए अपने पैरों पर चढ़कर
साढ़े पाँच फुट की ऊँचाई तक।
मर गए। ज़िन्दगी की इतनी ही ऊँचाई तक।
सिर झुकाकर कुछ इंच और कम हो गए।

There's only one tree left in the park,
or maybe the whole park's whitewashed on the tree.
The tree's like a government proclamation for a park.
Climbing trees is against the law,
so to honour it I climb onto my feet—
and reach 5'6".
Oi! Are these the great heights you've reached?
Mind your head and you're shorter by a few more inches.

मेरी एक अठन्नी
खो गई है।
मैं उसे ढूँढ़ता हूँ।
और मुझे मिल गया है
एक चाँदी का रुपया।
वह रुपया मेरा नहीं था।
परंतु उस रुपये में
मेरे कटे सिर का निशान है।
(क्या! मैं राजा बाबू हो गया था!
जबकि कटे सिर में मेरी, कंघी नहीं थी!)
वह रुपया मेरा नहीं था!
तो उस अठन्नी में ज़रूर मेरा धड़ होगा।
और इसलिए पूरी मेहनत से ढूँढ़ ही रहा हूँ
अपनी खोई हुई अठन्नी।
पर हाय! मुझे क्या पता था
कि मेरा अधूरा व्यक्तित्व
एक निन्यान्वे का फेर होगा।

My eight anna coin
is lost.
When I go looking for it
I find a silver rupee.
The rupee's not mine,
but stamped on it
is my severed head.
My torso must then be
in the eight anna coin,
which is why I've been
searching for it desperately.
Who knew
that my unfinished person
would turn into
this money chase?

बाज़ार की सड़क
व्यस्त आदमी
और उसके दोनों हाथों
गंदा झोला
कहीं फटा। एक ख़ाली और दूसरा भरा।
जिसके अंदर
आलू भाजी गरम मसाले की पुड़िया।
और मिर्चा
लाल या हरा।
काश! मैं!
दस रुपये का नोट बनकर
उसकी झोली में पनाह पाता।
मैं अपनी ही झोली में
घुसा हुआ था।

A street in the bazaar,
a busy shopper
carrying a soiled, frayed
bag in each hand, one empty,
the other full. In it,
potatoes, leafy vegetables,
a packet of garam masala,
and chillies,
both red and green.
How I wish I'd been
a ten rupee note
and sheltered in that bag,
but I was stuck
inside my own.

(1960)

एक छोटा कमरा
जिसमें तस्वीरें
सजाने के लिए
कई कीलें ठुकी हैं।
पर तस्वीरें तो कुछ भी नहीं
हाथ जहाँ तक
आसानी से पहुँचते हैं—
उन कीलों तक
उतरे कपड़े
सलीक़े से टँगते हैं।
ताकि दूसरे दिनों
उन्हें फिर से पहिना जा सके।

A small room
with many nails
hammered into the walls
to hang pictures from,
but there's not one
picture to be seen.
Hanging neatly
from the nails,
within easy reach,
are clothes
to be worn again
a few more times.

पेड़ की फटी खाकी वर्दी पहिन कर
ठूँठ यहाँ आकर खड़े हो गए हैं।
एक के बाद एक
लगातार
सैकड़ों क़तारें हैं।
इस तरह बगीचा है
या कोई फौजी टुकड़ी थक कर खड़ी है।
चारों तरफ़ लोहे के कँटीले तार का घेरा है।
कोई पेड़ बाहर निकल आए
या किसी के पेड़ तक जाने का डर!
सख्त पहरा!
शायद सब क़ैदी हैं।
या दुश्मनों का उजाड़ बगीचा है
हमारे क़ब्ज़े में।
मैं इतना थका हूँ
कि एक पेड़ से नहीं
एक बगीचे से पीठ टेक कर
सुस्ता रहा हूँ।
यह बगीचा मेरा नहीं है।

One behind the other, row after row,
dressed in the service khakis of trees,
stumps have come and stood here.
Is this an exhausted detachment of troops
or a park?
There's barbed wire fence on all sides.
No tree should escape,
or is there a fear that someone might approach them?
The security here is strict.
Perhaps this is a prisoner-of-war camp
or a devastated territory
that we occupy.
I'm so tired out
that when I rest my back
it's not against a tree
but the whole park.
This isn't my park.

(1966)

आकाश से उड़ता हुआ
एक छोटा सा हरा तोता
(गोया आकाश से
एक हरा अंकुर ही फूटा है।)
एक पेड़ में जाकर बैठ गया।
पेड़ भी ख़ूब हरा-भरा था।
फिर तोता मुझे दिखाई नहीं दिया,
वह हरा-भरा पेड़ ही दिखता रहा।

A small green parrot
flew down from the sky
(as if in the sky
a green shoot had appeared)
and settled on a tree.
The tree was luxuriantly green.
After this, I couldn't see the parrot.
Only the tree.

एक-एक सूखा पत्ता
ठहर-ठहरकर गिरता है।
पेड़ में यह कुछ इस तरह लगातार है।
कि मैं उस पेड़ को बड़बड़ाकर
घड़ी कह देता हूँ। कलाई पर बँधी घड़ी।
साथ वाला सुन लेता है।
समय देखने के लिए बहुत समय लगता है।
एक सूखा पत्ता गिरता है, जैसे एक सेकंड है।
यदि कोई पूछता है कि कितना बजा है
तो मैं ग़ुस्से से कह देता हूँ मुझे घड़ी, देखना नहीं आता।
घड़ी देखने से गर्दन झुकानी पड़ती है।
चाहे सामने एक शीशम का बड़ा पेड़ ही हो।
पूछने वाला अफसर लगता है।
एक कोंपल हरी पत्ती बजा दिया गया है जनाब!
वह बोलता है।
चाहे दो कोंपल हरी पत्ती बजा दिया गया हो। साथ वाला
बोलता है।
रिक्शा वाला पूछता है मोती बाग जाने के लिए।
साथ वाला कहीं चला गया।

Continuously,
at regular intervals,
one dry leaf after another
falls from the tree.
Which is why
I mutter under my breath
that the tree's a wristwatch.
A friend overhears me.
It takes time to tell the time.
A dry leaf falls
as though it were a second.
Asked the time, I shoot back,
'Don't know how to read it.'
A huge mahogany is ticking before you,
but to look at a watch you must still bend your neck.
The man who asked the time
looks like he's the big cheese:
'Hello, it's struck a new green leaf.'
'Does it matter if it's struck two?' the friend replies curtly.
'Anyone for Moti Park?' the rickshaw puller asks.
The friend is nowhere around.

(1964)

मुझे अपनी इस जालीदार खिड़की से
दूर तालाब का एक टुकड़ा तालाब दिखता है।
और आकाश का एक टुकड़ा आकाश
कुछ हरे-भरे पेड़।
इस तरह देखने से देखता हूँ
कि मेरी खिड़की की जाली
उस तालाब के पानी में
पेड़ों में
और आकाश में भी पड़ गई है।
अफ़सोस! तालाब की मछली
मेरी खिड़की की जाली में फँसी नहीं
और हरे-भरे पेड़ों का पक्षी
आकाश से उड़कर कहीं भी चला गया।
कमरा बंदकर इतनी तेज़ी से सीढ़ी उतरता हूँ
कि कमरे का सीढ़ियों से पीछे-पीछे
उतर आने का डर बहुत है।

Through the window screen,
of the distant pond, I can see
a fragment of the pond,
of the sky—a fragment of the sky,
and a few trees, luxuriantly green.
Seen from this angle, the window screen
has trapped the pond, the trees,
and the sky.
Tough luck. The fish in the pond
escape through the screen,
and the birds in the trees
disappear from the sky.
Locking the room, I flee down the stairs,
terrified that the room
is coming after me.

वह आदमी नया गरम कोट पहिन कर चला गया विचार की तरह

(1981)

That Man Put on a New Woollen Coat and Went Away Like a Thought
(1981)

आकाश की तरफ़
अपनी चाबियों का गुच्छा उछाला
तो देखा
आकाश खुल गया है।
ज़रूर आकाश में
मेरी कोई चाबी लगती है!
शायद मेरी संदूक की चाबी!

खुले आकाश में
बहुत ऊँचे
पाँच बममारक हवाई जहाज़
दिखे और छुप गए—
अपनी ख़ाली संदूक में
दिख गए दो-चार तिलचट्टे
संदूक उलटाने से भी नहीं गिरते!

When I tossed a bunch of keys
in the air,
I saw
the sky open.
Surely one of the keys
of my strongbox
opened it.

High up
in the clear sky
five fighter jets appear
and disappear,
and inside the strongbox
are a couple of cockroaches
that refuse to come out
even when the box is
held upside down.

(1965)

वृक्ष की सूखी
टहनियों के समानान्तर
मैंने अपनी
दो सुन बाँहें फैलाईं
और फुनगी पर एकटक दृष्टि

यह चाहता हूँ
कि जब पानी आए
तो पहले आँखें भिगो दे

फिर कोई चिड़िया
मेरी बाँहों की हरियाली में
घोंसले बनाए
अंडे दे।

My numb arms
are parallel
with the tree's
dry branches
and my eyes are fixed
on a leaf bud.

When it rains,
I want my eyes
to be wet first.

After that,
in the green
of my arms,
for a bird
to make a nest,
lay eggs.

(1960)

35

कुछ इस तरह याद नहीं
कि झाड़ी में
कहीं एक फूल होगा
पर दिखता नहीं
पास से भी नहीं।

इस तरह याद है
कि शायद फूल होगा
दूर से देखने पर भी फूल होगा।

मुझसे वह कितनी दूर है
अचानक भी नहीं देख पाता।

याद करने से मालूम पड़ता है
कि कितना भूल गया।

I don't seem to remember
if there was a flower in the bush.
I didn't see it,
not even from up close.

What I remember is
perhaps there was a flower
that was a flower
even when seen from afar.

From how far? I never came
even suddenly upon it to guess.

Trying to remember I realise
how much I forget.

(1978)

पाँच साल की सबसे छोटी लड़की
दौड़ते हुए मेरे पास आई
—दादा आपकी प्रेमिका आई।

पत्नी ने उसे अपने पास बैठाया
तब तक मैं
नीचे से भागकर
ऊपर दूसरे किरायेदार के पास चला गया
जैसे तराई से पहाड़ में।

ऊपर से मैंने बताया
कि मकान मालिक
किराया मैदान से पहाड़ का
पचास रुपया लेता है
अकेला था तब जैसे
पूरा प्रांत ख़ाली था
तब मकान मालिक
पूरे प्रांत का किराया
तीस रुपया लेता था।

पत्नी ने प्रेमिका से कहा
कि गुज़र हो जाती है
अब ऐसा लगता है
कि प्रांत में नहीं
बस किराये के मकान में रहते हैं
झाड़ू पोंछा प्रांत में नहीं

A five-year-old girl,
the youngest in the group,
came running to me.
Dada, she said, your beloved is here.

My wife made the visitor
sit down beside her
but I ran upstairs
where the other tenant lived.
It was like running
from the Terai to the mountains.

And from there I said to them,
the rent for this place,
from the Terai to the mountains,
is fifty rupees,
though when I lived here by myself,
in this whole province so to speak,
the landlord charged thirty.

We just about make do,
my wife said to my beloved.
We no longer now feel
that we live in a province
but in rented accommodations.
We sweep and mop the floor
not of a province but of our house.
We're a small family,

घर में लगाते हैं
गृहस्थी बहुत छोटी है
एक लड़का एक लड़की है
दुनिया से कोई मतलब नहीं है।

मैंने कहा कि मतलब है
पलस्तर घर का नहीं
प्रांत का झरता है
झंझट अपने रसोई-घर में ही नहीं
चूल्हे सबके हैं।

प्रेमिका उदास हो गई
गोया उसे भूख लग रही थी

घर में भी मुझे घर की याद आती है।

one son, one daughter,
and we don't have much
to do with the world.

Of course we do, I protested.
The plaster's coming off
not just of our house but of the province.
The problem's not in our kitchen alone.
Everyone has to cook.

My beloved became sad
as if she was hungry.

Even at home I miss my home.

(1976)

41

प्रकृति में
मैं शहरी आदमी
अजीब तरीक़े से खोया

बस में चढ़ने के लिए लोगों की लाइन
इस तरह लगती है
कि आदमियों के बीच
किनारे का पेड़ भी
लाइन में शामिल हो जाता है
उस पेड़ के पीछे अकेला मैं
सबसे पीछे।

बस के आने के बाद
मैं पढ़ा-लिखा समझदार
खड़ा रहा
कि बस में पेड़ चढ़े फिर उसके पीछे मैं
तब मुझे मालूम होता है
कि पेड़ बस में नहीं चढ़ता।

और मैं शहरी आदमी
प्रकृति से इस तरह अलग होता हूँ
कि पेड़ को पीछे छोड़ बस में बैठ जाता हूँ।

बस में बैठे मेरी इच्छा है
कि पूरे रास्ते में दोनों ओर पेड़ मिलते रहें

मैंने अपने कमरे में
पूरे जंगल की तस्वीर लगा रखी है।

A city person,
I was strangely disoriented
in the midst of nature.

In the bus queue
it looked as though
a roadside tree
had come and joined in too.
I was right behind it,
the last in line.

Now I'm an educated man.
When the bus arrived
I waited for the tree to get on first
when it struck me that trees
do not board buses.

And I who am a city dweller,
was separated from nature
in such a way that leaving the tree behind
I took my seat on the bus.

Once seated, my only wish
was to see trees on either side of the road
all the way back.

In my room I've hung a picture
of a whole forest.

(1976)

43

सब कुछ होना बचा रहेगा
(1992)

Everything to Be Done Will Remain to Be Done

(1992)

धौलागिरि को देखकर
मुझे याद आई
धौलागिरि की तस्वीर
क्योंकि तस्वीर पहले देखी गई थी।

पितामह पूर्वजों के भी चित्र हैं घर में
पूर्वजों को मैंने कभी नहीं देखा
मैं पूर्वजों को नहीं पूर्वजों के चित्र याद करता हूँ।

लेकिन धौलागिरि को देखने के बाद
मैं अपने पूर्वजों के चित्र नहीं
पूर्वजों को याद करता हूँ।

Seeing Mount Dhaulagiri,
I was reminded of its picture,
as I'd seen the picture first.

Among the pictures in my house
are portraits of my ancestors.
I haven't seen my ancestors,
so whenever I think of them
it's their portraits I think of.

But not after seeing Dhaulagiri.
Now it's the ancestors who come to mind
and not their likenesses.

समुद्र में जहाँ डूब रहा था सूर्य
इस तरह डूब रहा था
कि पश्चिम की दिशा भी उसके साथ
डूब रही थी
कि कल सूर्य के डूबने के लिए
पश्चिम की दिशा नहीं होगी
बाक़ी बची किसी दिशा में
वह डूबता है तो डूब जाए।

समुद्र में जहाँ उदित हो रहा है सूर्य
एक ऐसे समुद्री पक्षी की तरह
जो निकलने की कोशिश करता है
पर सतह के तेल से
पंख लिसटे होने के कारण
निकल नहीं पाता है।

इस न निकल पाने वाले सूर्योदय को देखने
न पर्यटकों की भीड़ थी
न पर्यटक आत्माओं की।

इस न निकल पाने वाले सूर्योदय के
दिन भर के बाद
न निकल पाने वाला सूर्य डूब जाता है।

The way the sun was going down
where it was going down
in the sea, the west was
going down with it, leaving
no west for tomorrow's sun
to go down into.
If it sets in some other direction,
then let it.

Where it rises in the sea,
the sun is like a sea bird
trying to rise,
but with the oil on the surface
sticking to its feathers,
it's unable to.

To watch the sunrise that is not a sunrise
there are no tourists
or tourist souls.

After a whole day of this sunrise
that is not a sunrise,
the sun, unable to rise, sets.

दूर से अपना घर देखना चाहिए
मजबूरी में न लौट सकने वाली दूरी से अपना घर
कभी लौट सकेंगे की पूरी आशा में
सात समुंदर पार चले जाना चाहिए।
जाते-जाते पलटकर देखना चाहिए
दूसरे देश से अपना देश
अंतरिक्ष से अपनी पृथ्वी
तब घर में बच्चे क्या करते होंगे की याद
पृथ्वी में बच्चे क्या करते होंगे की होगी
घर में अन्न जल होगा कि नहीं की चिंता
पृथ्वी में अन्न जल की चिंता होगी
पृथ्वी में कोई भूखा
घर में भूखा जैसा होगा
और पृथ्वी की तरफ लौटना
घर की तरफ लौटने जैसा।
घर का हिसाब-किताब इतना गड़बड़ है
कि थोड़ी दूर पैदल जाकर घर की तरफ लौटता हूँ
जैसे पृथ्वी की तरफ।

From a great distance you should see your home,
a distance from which, even if forced, you cannot return;
hoping always that one day you will
go where the seven seas take you.
Before leaving, turn back and see
your country from another country,
the earth from outer space,
so that when you're thinking of your children
and what they're busy with at home
you'll be thinking of the children of earth,
and the worry of supplies falling short at home
will be the worry of supplies falling short on earth,
a hungry person on earth
will be like a hungry person at home,
and returning to earth
will be like returning home.
Things at home are in such a mess that
after taking a few steps when I turn towards home
it's like turning towards the earth.

सूखा कुआँ तो मृत है
बहुत मरा हुआ
कि आत्महत्या करता है

अपनी टूटती मुंडेर से
अपनी गहराई भरता हुआ
कुएँ के खोदने से निकले हुए
पत्थरों से
जो मुंडेर बनी थी।

कुएँ के तल की कुआँसी इच्छा
उसकी अंदरूनी गहरी
बारूद से तड़कने की,
परंतु अपने ही निकले हुए पत्थरों और मिट्टी से
भरता हुआ कुआँ
कुआँ न होने की तरफ़ लौट रहा है,
अब यह पलायन था कुएँ का
गाँव पहले उजाड़ हो चुका था।

The dry well is dead,
so dead that it's become
suicidal.

The stones
of the broken parapet
with which it is filling its depth
are the ones that were removed
when it was dug.

Buried in its heart,
a well-like wish:
to explode like dynamite.
Instead, consuming itself
with its own rubble,
it's turning back
into what it was.
We're seeing the flight of the well.
The village had already been deserted.

एक सूखी नदी
दूसरे वर्ष भी सूखी रही
तो रेत के बहुत नीचे
वह और सूख जाएगी,
सूखी नदी के नीचे
सूखी नदी की परतें हैं।

कई वर्षों से ऐसी सूखी नदी के
किनारे के गाँव में
जैसे अंततः रहता हुआ
गाँव का सबसे बूढ़ा आदमी
नदी की रेत की तह से
आख़िरी में ढूँढ़ लेगा
एक पारदर्शी फॉसिल शिला
जिसमें चिन्हित होगी
नदी की वनस्पति
नदी की मछली
जीव, घोंघे
और शिला में बंद
एक बूँद पानी
जिसकी आयु करोड़ों वर्ष होगी—
सबसे बूढ़े आदमी के प्राणों में
धान का एक बीज सुरक्षित है।

A dry river
was dry again the following year.
Deep below,
it would've been drier.
Below dry rivers
are channels of more dry rivers.

In a village
along one such river
its oldest man,
the last one alive,
will eventually find
buried in the sediment
a transparent rock
in which are fossils
of river vegetation,
river fish,
organisms, and snails,
and also locked inside,
one drop of water
millions of years old.
Preserved in the soul of the oldest man
is a single seed of rice.

जाते-जाते ही मिलेंगे लोग उधर के
जाते-जाते जाया जा सकेगा उस पार
जाकर ही वहाँ पहुँचा जा सकेगा
जो बहुत दूर संभव है
पहुँचकर संभव होगा
जाते-जाते छूटता रहेगा पीछे
जाते-जाते बचा रहेगा आगे
जाते-जाते कुछ भी नहीं बचेगा जब
तब सब कुछ पीछे बचा रहेगा
और कुछ भी नहीं में
सब कुछ होना बचा रहेगा।

It's by going that you'll meet the others
It's by going that you'll arrive on the other shore
It's by going that you'll be able to reach there
Which looked impossible before
It's by going that you'll leave behind what's behind you
It's by going that what lies ahead will remain
It's by going that when there's nothing remaining
Everything behind you will still remain
And in the nothing that is still remaining
Everything to be done will remain to be done.

ज़मीन पर बैठा पक्षी
आकाश की तरफ़ उड़ता है
तो क्या उसे लगता है
कि वह धरती छोड़कर
पृथ्वी के ऊपर उड़ रहा है
पृथ्वी के ऊपर उड़ने के लिए
कितने ऊँचे जाना पड़ता होगा!

आकाश से आकर पक्षी
पेड़ पर बैठते हैं
तो क्या उन्हें लगता होगा
कि वे पृथ्वी पर जाकर बैठे हैं!

मेरे पंख नहीं हैं।

एक छोटी पीली तितली
पृथ्वी के ऊपर उड़ रही है।

Do birds sitting on the ground
feel that they've left the earth and are flying above it
when they climb the air?
To fly above it
you really have to go high.

And when they return
and sit on trees,
do birds feel
that it's the earth they're sitting on?

I don't have wings.

There's a small yellow butterfly
flying above the earth.

पेड़ के नीचे बैठना
अच्छा लगता है
अंदर की दुनिया में
जाने का रस्ता है।

अंदर की दुनिया में
अंदर का जंगल
जड़ ही जड़
जड़ों का जंगल
निकली जड़ें जड़ों से
उनसे भी निकली बस जड़।

जड़ की ऊँची शाखा पर
अंदर की चिड़िया बैठी
चहचह अंदर की।
खो गया
भटका जंगल में मैं दूर
घूमता इधर-उधर
ढूँढ़ा अपने को
उधर-इधर गुमसुम।

जड़ों में नहीं पत्तियाँ फूल
पतझड़ पसंद नहीं मुझको
पसंद
बसंत
इसीलिए दो-चार खिले
मेरे मन के फूल।

60

It feels good
to sit under a tree.
It leads to
the internal world.

In the internal world
is the internal forest.
Roots and more roots,
a forest of roots.
Roots growing out of roots,
with more coming out of them.

On the topmost branch
of a root
sits the internal bird
making internal sounds.
Seeking myself,
I keep losing my way
in the forest,
keep finding it.

There are in roots no flowers or leaves.
Spring is my season,
not autumn,
which is why a few flowers,
just one or two, the ones I wanted,
have bloomed.

बाहर की दुनिया में
लौटकर वापस आना
अच्छा लगता है।

पेड़ के नीचे बैठना
बाहर की दुनिया में
आने का रस्ता है।

It feels good
to be back
in the outside world.

To find
the way to it,
sit under a tree.

हिरन तेज़ दौड़ता है
कुलाँचे भी भरता है
जैसे जंगल के सींकचों के अंदर।

पक्षी उतनी दूर नहीं जाता होगा
जितनी दूर वह जा सकता है।
हिमालय उतना ऊँचा नहीं है
वह कुछ और ऊँचा हो सकता था।
समुद्र कुछ छोटा, कुछ कम गहरा है।
एक लंबी नदी, कुछ कम लंबी है।
तारे और हो सकते थे, कम हैं।

वह एक हवा है जो सब जगह है,
सब जगह का भी एक सींकचा है।

और यह वही हवा है
न उसमें कोई जोड़ है
और न उसमें कोई गठान है।
जेल से बाहर की साँस
कोई नहीं ले रहा है
जेल में नेल्सन मंडेला हैं।

Swiftly the deer runs, leaping
as though inside
the iron bars of a forest.

The bird doesn't seem to fly
as far as it can go,
the Himalayas are not as tall
as they could be,
the sea is a fraction too small, too shallow,
and the long river is a little less long.
There could be more stars.

There's one wind, it's the same wind everywhere,
just as every place has one iron bar.

And it's the same wind,
without joints or knots,
that you and I breathe.
No one's breathing
the air outside the prison.
Inside the prison is Nelson Mandela.

अंतिम चीता मरा
और चीता की जाति समाप्त हो गई
    मनुष्य से।

चीता शब्द है, पर चीता नहीं
चीते के चित्र और घटनाएँ, कहानियाँ
    हैं मनुष्यों में।

पृथ्वी से क्या कुछ नष्ट नहीं हो गया होगा
और वह सब कुछ है
जिससे नष्ट हो जाएगी पृथ्वी, पृथ्वी शब्द,
पृथ्वी चित्र, पृथ्वी घटनाएँ, पृथ्वी कहानियाँ
मनुष्य चित्र, मानुष कथा।

छुपाकर रख देना चाहिए
इस अमावस की आदिम गुफा में
स्त्री-पुरुष का प्रेम और सहवास।

भारत में चीता सन् 1952 से विलुप्त हो गया है।

The last cheetah is dead,
and one more species
      is extinct.

Cheetah is a word, but it's not a cheetah.
In news, pictures, and stories, the cheetah
      is among us.

There's no inventory of what the earth has lost,
yet everything remains that will kill the earth—
the word earth, earth's pictures, earth's news, earth's stories,
mankind's images, mankind's stories.

In the earliest cave of this night of the new moon
let us hide our love and lovemaking.

The cheetah has been extinct in India since 1952.

पानी गिर रहा है,
बरसात की जगह—
जहाँ मैं रह रहा हूँ
बरसात का मेरा घर
बरसात की मेरी सड़क
बार-बार भीगते हुए
बरसात का मूल निवासी।
अरी! बरसात की गीली चिड़िया
पंख फड़फड़ा
शाखा पर भीगते बैठी रह
अभी आकाश बरसात का है
पानी के बंद होते ही
बरसात से सब कुछ होगा निर्वासित
मैं भी!
अपने मूल निवास का यही तिलिस्म है।

It's water falling
instead of rain.
In the place where I stay,
my house is in rain,
my street is in rain;
getting wet repeatedly,
I'm the original resident of rain.
O rain-wet bird!
Flutter your wings
and keep sitting where you are.
More rain is in the forecast.
As soon as rainwater stops falling,
everything, even I, will disappear
from the rain.
Such is the tilisma of our native place.

नदी के कुछ अदृश्य खंडहर हैं जलवाष्प
इतिहास की नदी है, गंगा, ब्रह्मपुत्र, जमुना, व्यास
एक मनुष्य नदी में स्नान करता है
यह सभ्यता है
नदी के किनारे एक स्त्री कपड़े धोती है
यह सभ्यता है
एक मृत लड़का नदी में
संस्कार की तरह
प्रवाहित होता है
बरसात नदी के खंडहर का दृश्य है
जहाँ नदी नहीं है
बरसात में भीगना पर्यटन है।

A few of the river's shadowy ruins have turned to vapour.
It's the river of history, the Ganges, the Brahmaputra, the Yamuna,
    the Beas.
A person bathes in the river.
That's civilisation.
A woman washes clothes on the riverbank.
That's civilisation.
A boy's dead body, in the river,
is immersed like a last rite.
The rain is a picture of the river in ruins.
Where no rivers flow,
to get wet in the rain is tourism.

जब मैं भीमबैठका देखने गया
तब हम लोग साथ थे।
हमारे सामने एक लाश थी
एक खुली गाड़ी में।
हम लोग उससे आगे नहीं जा पा रहे थे।
जब मैं उससे आगे निकल गया
तब हम सब आगे निकल गए।
जब मैं भीमबैठका पहुँचा
हम सब भीमबैठका पहुँच गए।

चट्टानों में आदिमानव के फुरसत का था समय
हिरण जैसा, घोड़े, बंदरों, सामूहिक नृत्य जैसा समय।
ऊपर एक चट्टान की खोह से कबूतरों का झुंड
फड़फड़ाकर निकला
यह हमारा समय था पत्थरों के घोंसलों में—
उनके साथ
जब मैं लौटा
तब हम लोग साथ थे।
लौटते हुए मैंने कबूतरों को
चट्टानों के घोंसलों में लौटते देखा।

When I went to see Bhimbetka,
we went together.
Ahead of us was a dead body
being carried in an open vehicle.
We were unable to overtake it.
When I overtook it,
we were all able to overtake it.
When I reached Bhimbetka,
we all reached Bhimbetka.

In the rock shelters was early man's downtime,
a time like deer, like horses, like monkeys, a time like group
    dancing.
From a cave above us, a flock of pigeons
fluttered out—
it was now our time in the nest inside rocks.
When I returned with them
we returned together.
While returning, I saw the pigeons
returning to their nests in the rocks.

अतिरिक्त नहीं
(2000)

Nothing Surplus
(2000)

हताशा से एक व्यक्ति बैठ गया था
व्यक्ति को मैं नहीं जानता था
हताशा को जानता था
इसलिए मैं उस व्यक्ति के पास गया
मैंने हाथ बढ़ाया
मेरा हाथ पकड़कर वह खड़ा हुआ
मुझे वह नहीं जानता था
मेरे हाथ बढ़ाने को जानता था
हम दोनों साथ चले
दोनों एक-दूसरे को नहीं जानते थे
साथ चलने को जानते थे।

Defeated, the man sat down.
I did not know the man
but I knew defeat,
which is why going up to him
I extended my hand.
He held my hand and stood up.
He did not know me
but he knew my extended hand.
We walked side by side.
We did not know each other
but we knew how to walk together.

ईश्वर अब अधिक है
सर्वत्र अधिक है
निराकार साकार अधिक
हरेक आदमी के पास बहुत अधिक है।
बहुत बँटने के बाद
बचा हुआ बहुत है।
अलग-अलग लोगों के पास
अलग-अलग अधिक बाक़ी है।
इस अधिकता में
मैं अपने ख़ाली झोले को
और ख़ाली करने के लिए
भय से झटकारता हूँ
जैसे कुछ निराकार झर जाता है।

There's too much god.
Far too much.
The formless
has so many forms
that everyone has
an excess of them.
Even after it's divided up,
there's plenty left.
Different people,
different plenties.
In this plenitude,
to further empty it,
I give my empty bag
a hesitant shake,
afraid I'll shake out
some of the formless.

अब पहुँच ही गए हैं

भविष्य कितना निकट
कि ठीक अगला क्षण।
वर्तमान कितना अतीत
कि ठीक यही क्षण।

बहुत समीप के भविष्य
और बहुत समीप के अतीत को
इर्द-गिर्द लिए
रात में उपस्थित हूँ।

मेरा पुराना
घुन लगी लकड़ी की पेटी में
अतीत का विस्मृत कबाड़ है
और स्मृति में नया बहुत नया।

अब पहुँच ही गए हैं
इस समय रात्रि के आठ बजे होंगे
रुकने के लिए रात के समय में
एक जगह बनाना चाहता हूँ
परंतु समय इसे
यात्रा की रात बना देता है
और दिशा इसे अमावस।

न पहुँचने के अंत तक लगता है
कि अब पहुँच ही गए हैं
जैसे पहुँचने के अंत तक।

I'm about to arrive.

The future is so close
that it's the next moment,
the present so past
that it's exactly now.

Keeping the future
that's so close and the past that's so near,
I'm present in the night.

In my old trunk
that borers have tunnelled into,
is the junk of the past.
Recollected, it's dazzlingly new.

I've almost arrived.
The time should be around eight.
I want to make a place
where I can stay in the dark hours
but time has turned
this journey into night
and the direction has made it
the night of the new moon.

Until I arrive, it'll seem
that I've almost arrived,
as if I were arriving at the end of arriving.

तथा मैं परोक्ष हूँ—
मैं तुमसे कहूँगा।

मेरे कहे को नहीं
कहे की प्रतिध्वनि
तुम्हें सुनाई देगी।

तुम मुझसे कहोगे! और
तुम्हारे कहे को नहीं
उसकी प्रतिध्वनि सुनाई देगी।

कविता, मैंने अपने से कहा।
जो सुनाई देती है वह प्रतिध्वनि है
जिसे मैंने अपने से कहा।

So I'm not here,
I'll say to you.

You won't hear what I've said.
You'll hear the echo
of what I've said.

You'll say something in reply.
And I won't hear what you've said.
I'll hear the echo of what you've said.

Poetry, I say to myself.
What you hear is the echo
of what I say to myself.

बाज़ार से ख़रीदी गई है यह टँगी हुई रंगीन तस्वीर
सुंदर गोल-मटोल बच्चों की—
कि अपने घर के बच्चे इतने सुंदर नहीं होते,
वैसे जूते-कपड़े
और इतने स्वस्थ, गोल-मटोल भी नहीं होते।

बहुत बिकती हैं
इसी तरह बच्चों की तस्वीरें
इसे ख़रीद लेने का मन
पिता के मन जैसा
किसी का भी हो जाता है
घर-घर अब तो आम हुआ है।

दरअसल अपने-अपने बच्चों की
गुमसुम सब तरफ़ चिंता है।

This colourful picture
picked up in the bazaar
and hanging on the wall
is of chubby, pink-faced
children—so unlike our own,
who're neither as chubby,
nor as pretty, nor wear
such nice clothes.

These pictures sell a lot.
There's always someone in every family
who'll feel as a father feels
and bring one home.

The truth is, though no one says it,
they're all worried about their children.

उसने उसके स्पर्श का अनुमान लगाना चाहा
लगा कि अनुमान में स्पर्श का गुण आ रहा है
उसने अनुमान लगाया अग्नि
वह थोड़ा जल गया।
उसने अनुमान लगाया जल
वह थोड़ा भीगकर डूब गया।
उसने धूप का अनुमान लगाया
और उसने छुआ कि सूर्य को ढँके हुए बादल
हट गए हैं।
उसने अंतरिक्ष का अनुमान लगाकर
ऐसा गहरा स्पर्श किया
कि नक्षत्रों की बाढ़ में
वह थोड़ा डूबकर भीग गया।

जब उसने उसके स्पर्श का अनुमान लगाना चाहा
तब वह उसके स्पर्श का अनुमान
ठीक-ठीक नहीं लगा सका।

He wanted to guess what her touch was like
and in the guessing felt he'd got a sense of it.
He guessed fire
and got slightly burnt.
He guessed water
and got slightly wet, then he drowned.
He guessed how hot the sun was,
and as soon as he touched sunshine
the clouds covering the sun
moved away.
He guessed outer space,
but touched it so deeply
that almost drowning
in the flood of stars
he got wet.

When he tried to guess what her touch was like
he couldn't guess her touch
accurately.

हवा के झरोखे से झोंका आया
ढूँढ़कर आया।

आँधी में खो गया झोंका
कितनी बयार, पुरवाई से होकर
पछवाकर, हवा की सड़क पर
हवा का रिक्शा
हवा ने रिक्शा चलाया
रिक्शे में बैठ झोंका आया।

घंटी बजाकर नहीं
हवा की हेंडिल पर घंटी की जगह
उड़ता पपीहा
पियू! पियू! से
दूरी को सामने से हटाता
थोड़ा सा स्पर्श आया।

After much snooping,
through the wind's window
came a gust of wind.

Lost inside storms,
past east winds and west winds,
travelling on the wind's road
came the wind's rickshaw
pedalled by the wind
in which the wind was sitting.

On the wind's handlebar
no bell was seen ringing,
but the hawk-cuckoo's cooing
kept lessening the distance
as it went by, lightly touching
the skin.

प्रतिमाएँ पत्थर की हैं
मूर्तियों में आनंद पत्थर का
सुख पत्थर का है
इस सुख से मुस्कुराहट पत्थर की।
हमारी चितवन के सामने पत्थर है
परंतु सब कुछ सजीव
कि प्रतिमा के चितवन के सामने
हम दोनों पथराए
हमारे पथराने में मूर्तियों का सौष्ठव
मूर्तियों की नक्काशी
हम दोनों आलिंगन में पथराए।

The idols are of stone,
their bliss is of stone,
their happiness, their smile
of happiness, is of stone.
We glance a look at stone
but everything is so alive that
when the idols steal a glance
we turn to stone ourselves,
perfectly carved statues,
no detail missing,
we two in our stone embrace.

दीवाल में एक खिड़की रहती थी
खिड़की से एक दृश्य रहता था
एक झोंपड़ी, दो पगडंडी, एक नदी
और दो-एक तालाब रहते थे
एक आकाश के साथ सबका होना रहता था
लोगों का आना-जाना कभी-कभी रहता था
पेड़-पक्षी रहते थे
खिड़की से सब कुछ रहता था
नहीं रहने में एक खिड़की खुली नहीं रहती थी
रहने में एक खिड़की खुली रहती थी
खिड़की से हटकर दीवाल में एक आदमी रहता था।

There was a window that lived in a wall.
Because of that window, there lived a view:
a hut, two footpaths, a river,
a couple of ponds.
One sky served all of them.
People came and went.
There were trees, birds.
Everything lived in the window.
If nobody was around, the window remained shut.
If someone was there, the window was open.
To one side of it, in the wall, there lived a man.

आकाश धरती को खटखटाता है
(2006)

The Sky Knocks on the Earth
(2006)

इस मैदानी इलाक़े में इस साल भी
पहाड़ नहीं हैं
पहाड़ न जाने कब से वहाँ हैं, जहाँ वे हैं।
उन्हें अब हटकर होना चाहिए
मसलन विंध्याचल, मोटर स्टैंड या कचहरी से सटकर
गाँव की पाठशाला या खेत के पीछे सतपुड़ा केवल।
हिमालय वहाँ ज़्यादती है
जहाँ हिमालय नहीं है।
वह मैदान ज़्यादती है
जहाँ मैदान नहीं है।
टाटानगर ज़्यादती है
जहाँ टाटानगर नहीं है!
इस साल यह समतल विस्थापित हो हिमालय पर
तराई पर नहीं
चोटी पर इस मैदान का शिखर इलाक़ा हो।
भोपाल हो अब की साल
बॉकल, पनियाजोब के पास।
गंगा के किनारे से हटकर
काशी महानदी के पास।
गरियाबंद गंगा से,
चंडीगढ़ साँची से,
नाँदगाँव से फरीदकोट,
और मद्रास से जुड़ा हो मुरादाबाद
सब जगह इस तरह विस्थापित हो
सब जगह के पास
कि सब जगह हो सब जगह के पास
और अकाल, आतंक, दुकाल में अबकी साल
गाँव से एक भी विस्थापित न हो।

This year too in these plains
there are no mountains.
For centuries the mountains have stayed in one place;
it's time they moved.
The Vindhyas, for instance, should come closer
to the bus stand and law courts,
and the Satpuras should go behind
the village school or farm.
The Himalayas seem unfair
to a place that doesn't have the Himalayas;
this maidan seems unfair
to a place that doesn't have a maidan;
Tatanagar seems unfair
to a place that is not Tatanagar.
This year let this level ground be displaced
not to the Terai but the Himalayas,
the ground's highest point rising like a Himalayan peak.
Let's have Bhopal this year
near Bakal and Paniajob,
Varanasi on the banks of the Mahanadi,
Gariaband near the Ganges,
Chandigarh near Sanchi,
Nandgaon near Faridkot,
and Madras next to Moradabad.
All places should be displaced
and brought near all other places,
so that every place is near every other place
and not a single person is displaced
because of drought, terrorism, or war
from the village this year.

कभी के बाद अभी

(2012)

After Then Comes Now
(2012)

जो जगह तय हुई
उसी जगह मैं हूँ
और हमेशा से
आने-जाने वालों को
तक रहा हूँ
यह वही जगह है
जहाँ हम इकट्ठे होंगे
वैसे किसी भी जगह
हम इकट्ठे हो सकते हैं
और सभी जगह इकट्ठे हो सकते हैं
चाहे कहीं भी मिलें
हम इकट्ठे होने की जगह पर मिलते हैं।

I'm at the place
where it was decided I'll be
and from where I've always
been observing
those who go by.
This is where we'll gather,
though come to think of it
we could've gathered
at any place and there's no place
where we couldn't have gathered.
No matter where we meet,
we invariably meet at the place
meant for gathering.

अब इस उम्र में हूँ
कि कोई शिशु जन्म लेता है
तो वह मेरी नातिनों से भी
छोटा होता है।

जन्म के संसार में कोलाहल है—
किसी ने सबेरा हुआ कहा तो
लड़का हुआ सुनाई दिया,
सुबह हुई चिल्लाकर कहा तो
लड़की हुई की ख़ुशी लगती है।
मेरी बेटी की दो बेटियाँ हैं
सबसे छोटी नातिन जाग गई
जागते ही उसने सुबह को
गुड़िया की तरह उठाया
बड़ी नातिन जागेगी तो
दिन को उठा लेगी।

I've reached the age
when any child that's born
is even younger
than my granddaughters

There's much festivity in the birthing world
If someone says *It's morning*
it looks like someone's had a boy
If someone with great joy shouts
It's morning! it looks like the newborn's a girl

My daughter has two girls
The moment the younger one rises
she picks up the day that is a doll
When the elder one gets up
she'll lift the day itself

अभी तक बारिश नहीं हुई
ओह! घर के सामने का पेड़ कट गया
कहीं यही कारण तो नहीं।

बगुले झुंड में लौटते हुए
संध्या के आकाश में
बहुत दिनों से नहीं दिखे
एक बगुला भी नहीं दिखा
बचे हुए समीप के तालाब का
थोड़ा सा जल भी सूख गया
यही कारण तो नहीं।

जुलाई हो गई
पानी अभी तक नहीं गिरा
पिछली जुलाई में
जंगल जितने बचे थे
अब उतने नहीं बचे
यही कारण तो नहीं।

आदिवासी! पेड़ तुम्हें छोड़कर नहीं गए
और तुम भी जंगल छोड़कर ख़ुद नहीं गए
शहर के फुटपाथों पर अधनंगे, बच्चे-परिवार
के साथ जाते दिखे
अपना जंगल नहीं इस साल
कहीं यही कारण तो नहीं।

It hasn't rained yet.
The tree in front of our house
had been cut down.
Is that the reason?

I haven't seen herons
returning in the evening.
It's been a while since I saw one.
The little water there was
in the nearby pond
has dried up.
Is that the reason?

July's come and gone,
and still no rain.
The forest that was there last July
has shrunk.
Is that the reason?

O adivasis! The trees did not desert you,
nor did you leave the forest on your own.
I saw groups of you walking down city streets this year,
bedraggled children in tow, forest people without forests.
Is that the reason?

इस साल का भी अंत हो गया
परंतु परिवार के झुंड में अबकी बार
छोटे-छोटे बच्चे नहीं दिखे
कहीं यह आदिवासियों के अंत होने का
सिलसिला तो नहीं।

The year's now ended.
In the groups of families
I noticed there were no infants.
Is this the beginning
of the end of the adivasis?

शहर से सोचता हूँ
कि जंगल क्या मेरी सोच से भी कट रहा है
जंगल में जंगल नहीं होंगे
तो कहाँ होंगे?
शहर की सड़कों के किनारे के पेड़ों में होंगे।

रात को सड़क के पेड़ों के नीचे
सोते हुए आदिवासी परिवार के सपने में
एक सल्फी का पेड़
और बस्तर की मैना आती है
पर नींद में स्वप्न देखने की
उनकी आँखें फूट गई हैं।

परिवार का एक बूढ़ा है
वह अभी तक देख सुन लेता है
पर स्वप्न देखते हुए आज
स्वप्न की एक सूखी टहनी से
उसकी आँख भी फूट गई।

When I think of forests
from the city, I could be killing
forests with a thought.
If not in the forest, where will forests be?
They'll be among city trees.

To an adivasi family
sleeping under roadside
trees at night, Bastar's
mynah bird and salfi palm
appear in a dream but the eyes
that see dreams are blind.

The family's oldest member,
who is still able to see and hear,
was today, while dreaming, struck in the eye
by a dry branch of the dream,
and he, too, lost his vision.

कोई अधूरा पूरा नहीं होता
और एक नया शुरू होकर
नया अधूरा छूट जाता
शुरू से इतने
कि गिने जाने पर
गिनती अधूरी छूट जाती

परंतु,
इस असमाप्त-अधूरे से भरे जीवन को
पूरा माना जाए, अधूरा नहीं
कि जीवन को भरपूर जिया गया

इस भरपूर जीवन में
मृत्यु के ठीक पहले भी मैं
एक नई कविता शुरू कर सकता हूँ
मृत्यु के बहुत पहले की कविता या
जीवन की अपनी पहली कविता की तरह।

किसी नए अधूरे को अन्तिम न माना जाए।

Nothing unfinished is completed
but a new beginning is made
and a new unfinished left behind.
They are now so many
you cannot finish counting them.

But look upon this unfinished life
filled with the incomplete
as a completed whole,
not one that you cannot
live abundantly.

In this abundant life,
in the moment before death,
a new poem could begin,
like the one begun years ago,
like the first poem you wrote.

No new unfinished should be seen as the last.

जन्म के साथ एक न एक दिन मृत्यु—
एक जुड़वाँ जन्म है।
मैं जन्मजात मृत्यु लिए फिरता हूँ।
जितने दिन जीवित रहूँगा
अपनी मृत्यु को बचाकर रखूँगा।
परंतु मृत्यु के बाद
गुल्लक में कहीं जीवन जमा रहता है।

गुल्लकों का खजांची बना फिरता हूँ
उनके भी गुल्लक का।

With birth is born its twin, death—
it's a double birth.
Wherever I go, I carry this inborn death with me.
I'll save it
for as long as I live.
But after death, somewhere in the piggy bank,
you'll find that life's been saved.

I walk around as though I were the treasurer of piggy banks,
even of their piggy banks.

जगह-जगह रुक रही थी गाड़ी
बिलासपुर में समाप्त होने वाली
'छत्तीसगढ़ एक्सप्रेस' में सवार था।
अचानक गोंदिया में
सभी यात्री उतर गए
और कलकत्ता तक जाने वाली
खड़ी दूसरी गाड़ी में चढ़ गए।
एक मुझसे भी अधिक बूढ़े यात्री ने
उतरते हुए कहा—
'तुम भी उतर जाओ,
अब अगले जनम पहुँचेगी यह गाड़ी।'

मुझे जल्दी नहीं थी
मैं गाड़ी में बैठा रहा
दो-चार स्टेशन बाद मुझे राजनाँदगाँव उतरना था
जहाँ मेरा जन्म हुआ था।

The Chhattisgarh to Bilaspur
on which I was travelling
would stop unwontedly.
Suddenly, at Gondia,
everyone disembarked
and rushed towards the Calcutta train
that had arrived.
Getting off, a passenger,
he was older than me, said,
You better get off too,
or you'll be waiting until your next life
for this one to reach its destination.

In no great hurry,
I was happy to be sitting where I was.
I was only going up to Rajnandgaon,
a few stations away,
where I was born.

मैं बाहर खड़ा रहा
मंदिर जाकर वह मूर्ति देखती है।

जब वह मंदिर से बाहर आई
तब मैं इधर-उधर चला गया
फिर दिखा
'कहाँ चले गए थे?'
'कहीं नहीं।'
मंदिर के बाहर उसके साथ रहा मैं।

मंदिर के अंदर
मूर्ति के साथ मूर्ति छूट गई।

I stood outside.
She went in to look at the idol.

When she came out
I wasn't around,
then she saw me.
'Where did you go?'
'Nowhere. I was here.'
I am with her outside the temple.

Inside the temple is the idol
left behind with the idol inside.

पैदल अपने पड़ोस जा रहा हूँ
इस तरह जाना क्या यात्रा नहीं है
बहुत दूर जाना ही यात्रा है
घर से निकला हूँ
अब पड़ोस जा रहा हूँ
दो क़दम ही चला हूँ
घर से दूर
मैं यात्रा में—
तीर्थ-यात्रा में।

I step out to go to a neighbour's.
Isn't this going on a journey?
To go on one must you always go far?
I've stepped out of my house
and am now going to a neighbour's.
My house is behind me.
I've taken two steps
of the journey—
the pilgrimage.

हम सब एक जगह एक साथ रहे होते
चूल्हे भी अलग नहीं होते घर के अंदर
उसी घर में जहाँ बाबा, अजिया,
पिता, चाचा और बहन-भाई रहे
वही पड़ोस भी रहा होता
प्रकृति रहती है प्रकृति के पड़ोस में
घास के पड़ोस में घास
मिट्टी के पड़ोस में मिट्टी
हवा में आँधी, तूफ़ान और
सुगंध से भरे झोंके रहते हैं
हवा कहीं टूटती नहीं
सारे संसार की हवा
बिना गाँठ के एक रहती है—
हमारी साँस के साथ।

Would that we all had lived together
under one roof,
without separate kitchens—
grandfather, great aunt,
father, uncle, siblings—
and stayed in the same neighbourhood.
Nature lives beside nature,
grass next to grass,
mud next to mud,
and in the wind live
storms, hurricanes, and scent-laden gusts.
Without knots,
there's one wind circling the earth,
together with our breathing.

जब बाढ़ आई
तो टीले पर बसा यह घर भी
डूब जाने को
आस-पास का सब पड़ोस इस घर में
मैं इस घर को धाम कहता हूँ
और ईश्वर की प्रार्थना में नहीं
एक पड़ोसी की प्रार्थना में
अपनी बसावट में आस्तिक हूँ
कि किसी अंतिम पड़ोस से भी
क्षितिज के पार से
एक पड़ोसी सबको उबारने
एक डोंगी लेकर चल पड़ा है।

इस टीले के ऊपर शिखर पर
मंदिर की तरह
एक और पड़ोसी का घर है।

In time of floods
even the house on the hillock
isn't safe.
Everyone in the neighbourhood gathers there.
The place, like a shrine.
I've little faith in god,
more in a neighbour's prayers
that a neighbour would have set out
from the last neighbourhood
across the horizon
in a small open boat to save us.

On top of the hillock
is the house of another neighbour
like a temple.

हो सकता है मरा न होऊँ
सब के समझने के बाद
जब धीरे से अपनी आँख खोलूँ
तो क्या दूसरे जनम जैसा मैं संसार को देखूँ
बुरे लोगों को तो भूल चुका होऊँगा
अच्छे लोग मुझे याद रहेंगे।
पहले भी यह संसार
आसपास-पड़ोस से याद रहा
और कोई एक चेहरा
मुझे याद दिला देता
कि मैंने संसार को नहीं छोड़ा।

थोड़े से में रहकर
थोड़े से को देखकर
थोड़े लोगों से मिलकर
थोड़े समय में पूरा समय
मेरा सब पड़ोस में रखा मिल जाएगा।

पहले भी चार-एक दिन के लिए
घर छोड़कर गया तो
कुछ काँसे-पीतल के बर्तन
एक चाँदी की अँगूठी, कुछ चिट्ठियाँ
एक टिन की पेटी में रखकर
पड़ोस में सुरक्षित छोड़ जाता था।

When everyone thinks I'm dead,
it may be I'm still alive,
and if I were to slowly open my eyes
the world would appear as to one reborn.
I will have forgotten the wicked,
remembered the good.
Even earlier, I'd recognise this world
from what was around me,
a familiar face
would remind me
that I was still alive.

Living with little,
having seen little,
friends with few people,
in a little time is all of time.
There is nothing of me except what is here.

Even earlier, going out for a few days,
I'd put the brass utensils,
the silver ring, and some letters
inside a tin trunk and leave it
with a neighbour
for safekeeping.

कुछ-कुछ याद करते
जीवन रोज़ बीतता रहा
सब भुला नहीं सका
जो याद रहता है
उसी से कुछ भुला देता हूँ
जो भुला देता हूँ
उसमें से याद कर लेता हूँ
और अपने होने को
काम की तरह सोचता हूँ
सोमवार से इतवार तक
एक तारीख़ से इकत्तीस तारीख़ तक
अगर बत्तीस होगी तो भी।

Things half remembered
The days slip by
Not everything is forgotten
From what is recalled
Something is forgotten
And from what is forgotten
Something is recalled
I look upon this
As a full-time job
From Monday to Sunday
From the first to the thirty-first
Even to the thirty-second
If there was one

कविता लिखते समय
मेरा ध्यान दुनियादारी में रहता है।

लिखते समय
कोई घर का बंद दरवाज़ा
खटखटाता है
तो मैं सुन लेता हूँ
और दरवाज़ा खोलता हूँ।

यह सच है
तब कोई आया होता है
भले किसी का पता पूछने
उसे मेरा ही घर आसान लगा हो
और उसने मेरा दरवाज़ा खटखटाया।

यह भी सच है कि
अपना दरवाज़ा खोलने पर
कविता इसी सजगता में आती है
और पता बताने पर
वह मेरा ही पता होता है।

Writing a poem,
worldly matters occupy me.

If I'm writing
and there's a knock on the door,
I go open it
when I hear the sound.

It's true that someone's there,
even if it is to look for an address,
and since my house looked approachable
knocked on the door.

It's also true that the alertness
that made me open the door
is the same that alerts me to a poem.
The address I'm shown
turns out to be mine.

(2008)

कहने को बहुत रहा
इतने बरस
कि अभी भी कहने को
कहने को मेरा पुकारना
पुकारना कहने को।

सुनने नहीं
चले जाने आया
आया नहीं जैसे।

जाना याद है
अभी गया
अभी भी चला जा रहा जैसे।

सब कहना
उसके पीछे चला गया
पुकारना रह गया
यहीं दहलीज़ पर।

For all these years
there was much to say.
There's much still left.
It was me calling out,
so it will seem.

It wasn't to listen,
I came here to leave.
As if I never came.

I remember the leaving.
I'm leaving this minute.
As if the leaving never stopped.

All that was said
left with the leaving.
What was left was the calling out,
here on the threshold.

कौन है?
पूछकर मैं हतप्रभ हूँ
कोई नहीं है—यह मैं ही उत्तर देता हूँ

मैं और मैं दोनों बात करते हैं
कि उम्र के समय को काट लूँ
आज, कल, आजकल काट लूँ
देर तक बात करते हैं
कि आज दिन कौन सा है?

आज दिन कौन सा है
बीत जाता है।

'Who's there?'
I ask, and my face turns pale.
'There's no one', is the answer I get.
I'm the one giving it.

We two, I and I, in old age,
are having a conversation
to pass the time,
pass the todays and tomorrows.
To know what day of the week it is
we spend long hours talking.

The day of the week that's today
has passed.

प्रतिनिधि कविताएँ

(2013)

Selected Poems
(2013)

भोपाल जाते हुए
छत्तीसगढ़ राज्य बनने के बाद
यह नहीं लग रहा है
कि मध्यप्रदेश जा रहे हैं
संक्षिप्त में म.प्र.
कोष्ठक का (म.प्र.) भी नहीं
भोपाल जाते हैं
प्रांत नहीं, प्रांत जाकर क्या करूँगा
और लौटकर रायपुर आते हुए
रायपुर आऊँगा।

हम हमेशा अपने होने के मुहल्ले में होते हैं
अपने होने के मुहल्ले में
नागपुर-भोपाल है
एक दिल्ली
एक रायपुर, एक नाँदगाँव
एक जगतपुर, एक घर
कोष्ठक में अन्तरिक्ष की
पूरी एक ख़ाली जगह।

छत्तीसगढ़, पहले मध्यप्रदेश का हिस्सा था, जो 1 नवंबर सन् 2000 को उससे अलग होकर नया राज्य बना।

After Chhattisgarh became a state,
when I went to Bhopal
it didn't seem that I was going to Madhya Pradesh,
abbreviated to M.P.,
or to put it in parentheses, even to (M.P.).
We go to Bhopal,
we don't go to a state.
And what will I do by going to a state?
And when I return to Raipur,
I'll return to Raipur.

We live in the precinct of ourselves,
and in that precinct
are Nagpur and Bhopal,
there is a Delhi,
a Raipur, a Nandgaon,
a Jagatpur, a house,
and in the empty space between parentheses,
is the cosmos.

(March 2001)

Chhattisgarh, which had been a part of Madhya Pradesh, was formed as a separate
state on 1 November 2000.

नई एवं असंग्रहीत कविताएँ

New and Uncollected Poems

अपनी भाषा में शपथ लेता हूँ
कि मैं किसी भी भाषा का
अपमान नहीं करूँगा
और मेरी मातृभाषा
हर जन्म में बदलती रहे
इसके लिए मैं बार-बार
जन्म लेता रहूँ—
यह मैं जीव-जगत से कहता हूँ
चिड़ियों, पशुओं, कीट पतंगों से भी।

I solemnly pledge
in my language
that I shall not insult anyone else's,
and so that I change
my language with every birth,
I pledge to keep being reborn.
I say this to the living world,
even to birds, animals, insects.

इस हो रही बारिश की
पहली बूँद कौन सी थी
कहाँ गिरी
यह कौन बताए
बारिश की बूँदों को गिनना बाक़ी है
और कोई पर भरोसा है।

इस जंगल का पहला उगा पेड़ कौन सा है
फिर दूसरा, तीसरा, सब गिना दे
इस पेड़ की पत्तियों में
पहली उगी पत्ती कौन सी है
कुल कितनी पत्ती हैं?

पहला सवाल दुनिया का
आख़िर क्या था
उत्तर क्या उसका मिला
जो सही न होकर
पहला ग़लत उत्तर ज़रूर हुआ होगा
वह क्या है?

पहली कौन सी भाषा का था पहला शब्द
फिर दूसरे, तीसरे शब्दों का
पहला वाक्य क्या था?
क्या कहा गया होगा!
जो पहले सुना वाक्य होगा
और पहले लिखने वाले ने
उसे पहले पढ़ा
सुनाया होगा!
कौन था वो, कौन बताए।

Of the rain that is falling,
which was the first drop?
Where did it fall?
Who has the answer?
The raindrops remain to be counted.
I trust someone will count them.

In the forest, which was the first tree,
the second, the third, and so on to the last?
Of this tree's leaves,
which was the first,
and how many leaves does it have?

What, after all, was the first question
that anyone asked,
and what was the answer?
Being the wrong answer,
it must've been the first wrong answer given.
What was it?

Of which first language was the first word,
followed by the second, the third,
to make the first sentence?
What was said in it?
The first sentence that was heard,
would have first been read to a listener
by the first person who wrote it.
Who was that person? Who's to tell?

शहर में इतनी भीड़ रहती है
कि जुलूस दिखाई नहीं देता
कभी लगता भीड़ बढ़ गई
या मैटनी शो छूटा
वैसे भी जुलूस
जनता का नहीं होता था
ट्रकों, बसों से आए लोगों से
भीड़ बढ़ जाती थी।

भीड़ से जनता को घटा दो
तो जनता अकेली एक बचती।
मैं जनता से जाकर मिलता
तो गिनती में दो होता।
सड़क पर दोनों दो के जुलूस में मिलते
लोगों के सुख-दुख की बात करते
भीड़ के हल्ले में
कभी ज़ोर से नारों में बात करते।

There's always such a crowd in the city
that the procession gets lost inside it
Sometimes it seems the crowd has grown
to be the crowd from the matinee show
The procession, in any case,
was never made of common people
Most of them are ferried in trucks and buses
to swell the numbers

Subtract the people from the crowd
and you'll be left with a people of one
I go and meet the people
and can count those I meet on my fingers
They're a procession of two
They talk of their joys and sorrows
Caught up in the noisy crowd
they even shout slogans

सबके साथ
अपने पैरों से नहीं
सबके पैरों से चल रहा हूँ
सबकी आँखों से देख रहा हूँ
जागता हूँ तो सबकी नींद से
सोता हूँ तो सबकी नींद में
मैं अकेला नहीं
मुझमें लोगों की भीड़ इकट्ठी है
मुझे ढूँढ़ो मत
मैं सब लोग हो चुका हूँ
मैं सबके मिल जाने के बाद
आख़िरी में मिलूँगा
या नहीं मिलूँगा
मेरे बदले किसी से मिल लेना।

Not with my own feet
but everyone's,
I'm walking with everyone,
seeing with everyone's eyes.
When I wake, it's from everyone's sleep,
when I sleep, it's under everyone's eyelids.
Far from being alone,
I'm a large gathering, and I'm each person in it.
Don't go looking for me.
If you find me, it'll be
after you've found everyone else.
Maybe you won't find me at all.
Instead of me, you can meet
the first person you see.

अब मैं उठने के लिए
केवल नींद पर भरोसा करता हूँ
अपनी नींद पर
किसी दूसरे पर नहीं
जब उठना होता है तो
नींद खुल जाती है
जागना चाहता हूँ तो नींद नहीं आती
रात भर जागूँ तो रात भर नींद नहीं आएगी
जब नहीं सोता तो
जम्हाई भी नहीं आती
नींद के भरोसे को आज़माने के लिए
बक़ायदा बिस्तर बिछाकर
मच्छरदानी लगा लूँगा
ओढ़ने के लिए चादर की ज़रूरत पड़ेगी तो
चादर भी रख लूँगा
तब भी मुझे नींद नहीं आएगी
और नींद पर मुझे भरोसा है
इसलिए मैं सबके लिए कहता हूँ
नींद तुम रात के अंत तक रहना
और रात तुम भी तब तक रहना
जब तक थके-माँदों की नींद रहे।

To get out of bed in the morning,
I don't depend on anyone
except on my sleep.
If I'm fast asleep
and it's time to get out of bed,
I find myself opening my eyes.
When I want to stay awake, sleep won't come.
If I stay awake all night sleep won't come all night.
When I don't sleep
I don't even yawn.
To put my confidence in sleep to the test,
I make my bed meticulously,
string up the mosquito net,
keep a sheet if I need one to cover myself,
and I still won't be able to sleep.
My confidence in sleep is unshaken.
Which is why I say on everyone's behalf,
Sleep, you stay on till the end of night,
and Night, you stay on too,
for as long as those who are tired out are sleeping.

आज कहीं नहीं जा सकता
सोचकर
आज का क़ैदी हो गया
चाहे अपने घर पर रहूँ
मैं अपने घर में भी क़ैद नहीं हो सकता
मैं पड़ोस तक जाता हूँ
जैसे चिड़िया पास के पेड़ पर
उड़कर चली गई
घर से बाहर की मेरी पहली स्वतंत्रता पड़ोस है
फिर पड़ोस के पड़ोस
और मैं आकाश में उड़ते पंछियों के
साथ-साथ चहकता हूँ।

I can't go out today.
The moment I say this
I become today's prisoner.
Even if I'm at home,
I'm not in a jailhouse.
Like a bird that flies to a nearby tree,
I step out into the neighbourhood,
then into the neighbourhood's neighbourhood,
and soon, tasting freedom,
I'm flying with the birds in the sky,
singing with them.

आदिवासी नाचते दिखते नहीं
नचाए जाते दिखते हैं
जो उनका घर है
उसमें वे रहते नहीं
वे दिखाने के घर हैं
उनका जो चूल्हा जल रहा है
यह उन्होंने नहीं जलाया
जलता हुआ दिखाने का है

जो कुछ दिखता है
वह दिखाने से दिखता है
और जो नहीं दिख रहा
छुपाने से नहीं दिख रहा
नहीं देख सकने वाले—
अंधे लोगों के लिए शहर में
जंगल की प्रदर्शनी लगी।

You don't see adivasis dancing
You see them being made to dance
Their houses are not
the houses they live in
Their houses are there to be displayed
The brick stove you see
is not what they've lit
It's been lit for others to look at

What you see
is because it is shown you
and what you don't see
is because it is hidden
For those who cannot see
they've put up an exhibition
of the forest in the city

जंगल से बाहर हुआ
एक आदिवासी आदमी
दूसरे आदमियों की तरह
सब तरफ़ दिखने लगा है
सब आदमी की तरह
भूखा सब लोगों की तरह
और पेट नहीं भर पा रहा
सब आदमी से बदतर
एक आदिवासी
कहीं भी आदिवासी नहीं
चलते-चलते राह के एक पेड़ के नीचे
खड़ा हुआ नहीं,
दूर चलते-चलते
दूसरे पेड़ के नीचे,
थककर भी बैठा नहीं,
जंगल से बाहर हुआ आदिवासी
एक पेड़ के लिए भी आदिवासी नहीं।

Take the adivasi
away from the forest
and he looks like
everyone else
He goes hungry
like everyone else
only the hungry
are better off
The adivasi
is nowhere an adivasi
Always on the road
he comes to a tree
and doesn't stop
He comes to another
and doesn't sit down
Take the adivasi
away from the forest
and he's not an adivasi
for even a tree

कोई भटक कर
आई किरण
मेरे चारों ओर के अंधेरे को
छेदने का प्रयत्न करे
तो मैं यह नहीं चाहता
मैं तो चाहता हूँ
कि मेरा अंधेरा
किरणों को भटकने न दे।

For a ray of sunlight
that has lost its way
to come and try
and make holes in the darkness around me
is not what I want,
but that my darkness
not let the ray of sunlight go astray.

(1960)

छोटी सी ख़ुशी जो मुझे मिलती है
लगता है मेरी अमीरी है
इसे सबको लुटा दूँ
या जमा कर दूँ पत्नी के पास
थोड़ा-थोड़ा जेब ख़र्च के लिए
उसी से ख़ुशी माँग लूँगा।

Any little happiness
is like wealth to me,
to give away freely
or to deposit it with my wife.
Needing a little happiness,
I'll ask her for pin money.

हम दोनों बूढ़े हो गए
थके रहते
घुटनों में तकलीफ़ रहती
ज़मीन पर बैठने का मन करता
पर बैठ नहीं पाते
मैं बैठ जाता तो
उठ नहीं पाता

चलने फिरने में
इतने धीमे हो गए
कि छोटा घर
बड़ा लगता

हम आस-पास होते
एक-दूसरे को वहीं ढूँढ़ते
और वहीं मिल जाते

तब प्यार से मैं उसे
पहले की तरह
कह देता हूँ
तुम बहुत अच्छी लड़की हो
वह भी कहती है कि
मैं बहुत अच्छा लड़का हूँ।

We've both become old
We tire easily
The knee joints are stiff
I like to sit on the floor
but cannot
And once I sit down
I'm unable to get up

My movements
are so slow
that even a small house
seems large

Never far from each other
we look for each other
and find each other
right here

Then with the same affection
as before
I say to her
You're a lovely girl
and she with the same affection says
You're a lovely boy

बच्चों की कविताएँ

Poems for Children

शब्द अर्थ कथा

एक
तैरना—एक शब्द पानी में तैरता दिखता है
डूबना—एक शब्द पानी में डूब जाता है
सहायता—एक शब्द के साथ वह शब्द तैरते
डुबकी लगाकर उसे बचाता है।

दो
पेड़ शब्द के नीचे
एक शब्द छाया
उड़कर शब्द पक्षी
पेड़ शब्द पर जा बैठा।

Word Meaning Story

One

Swimming—A word is seen swimming in water
Drowning—A word drowns in water
Help—With another word, this word dives into the water and saves
  it.

Two

Under the word tree
A word shade
When it flies, word is bird
Sitting atop the word tree

कटे हुए पेड़ के ठूँठ
जंगल कटने के क़दम हैं।

Those tree stumps are the footsteps
of a destroyed forest.

चित्र कविता

एक शब्द (चिड़िया) कोष्ठक के घोंसले में।

Picture Poem

A word
      (bird)
in a parenthetical
      nest

मैंने कहा जिराफ़ से—
करो तुम पहले
अपनी गर्दन नीचे
ताकि मैं हो सकूँ सवार गर्दन पर
दोनों कान पकड़कर।

मैं जाँच करूँगी
एक-एक चिड़ियों के घोंसलों की
कि जिराफ़ खाता है
पत्ती
घोंसले बचा के या उजाड़ के!

एक भी चिड़िया ने
यदि की शिकायत मुझसे
मैंने कहा उससे
तो! जिराफ़—
दोनों कान मैं तुम्हारे
मरोड़ दूँगी कसके!

I said to the giraffe,
You first lower your neck
for me to grab your ears
and sit on your back.

I want to look into
every bird's nest
and make sure
that when you eat leaves
you don't also break birds' eggs.

If even one bird
reports you,
I said to the giraffe,
I'll twist both your ears
really hard.

और नाम का गोंद

काग़ज़ के टुकड़ों को
जोड़कर लंबा करने
गोंद लगाते हैं।
वाक्य को लंबा करना हो तो
और लगाते हैं।

The Glue Called *and*

To join and make longer
pieces of paper
you use glue.
To make sentences longer
you use *and*

मैदान की मिट्टी से खेल रहा था
दरअसल मैदान से खेल रहा था,
हाथ, पैर, कपड़ों में
मिट्टी लग गयी थी—मैदान लग गया
चोट भी लगी, मैदान से लगी
मुट्ठी में मिट्टी को लिया—
मैदान का टुकड़ा लिया
मिट्टी जेब में डाली—
थोड़ा मैदान जेब में डाला, चला
और थोड़ी सी मिट्टी जाकर
कमरे में रख दी
थोड़ा सा मैदान रख दिया।
पर इससे मैदान इतना
सुनसान हो गया
कि मैदान में मैदान नहीं था
मैदान से मैदान भी चला गया।

I was mucking around in the maidan
Actually, I was playing in the maidan
I had dirt all over me
I had the maidan on my hands and feet, on my clothes
Even if I was bruised, I was bruised by the maidan
I picked up a handful of dirt
I picked up a piece of the maidan
I put the dirt in my pocket
I put a little maidan in my pocket, and left
I went and kept
a little dirt in my room
a little maidan in my room
But this made the maidan
so desolate
that there was no maidan in the maidan
The maidan went away even from the maidan

किसकी कमी है?
जो है नहीं
उसकी कमी है

और जो कम है
उसकी कमी है

जो ज़्यादा नहीं
उसकी कमी है

जो ज़्यादा है
और ज़्यादा नहीं
उसकी कमी है

तो ज़्यादा क्या है?
कमी कम नहीं
वही ज़्यादा है।

What's fallen short?
What we don't have
has fallen short

and what is less
has fallen short.

What is not in excess
has fallen short

and what is more
but is not more
has fallen short.

What is more, then?
The fallen short that has never fallen short
is more.

Acknowledgements

Grateful acknowledgement is made to the editors of the following publications where some of these translations first appeared: *Almost Island, Granta, Metamorphoses, Modern Poetry in Translation, Plume, Some Kind of Beautiful Signal* (eds. Jeffrey Yang and Natasha Wimmer), *The Baffler, The Common,* and *Words Without Borders.*

I am grateful to Bob and Susan Arnold of Longhouse Poetry for bringing out a selection of these poems in a limited edition.

Sara Rai helped me find the right words for some of the originals, some of which Shashwat Gopal helped me trace. Shashwat also provided the files of the Hindi text. I remain grateful to them both.

Translation is all about getting the original wrong. How wrong is up to the translator. I alone am responsible for any errors.

9 789360 458751

Printed by Libri Plureos GmbH in Hamburg, Germany